WHEN GOD ENLARGES YOUR HEART

WHEN GOD ENLARGES YOUR HEART

Finding Room in Your Heart to Grow

Amy Hopkins Gilbride

WHEN GOD ENLARGES YOUR HEART
Finding Room in Your Heart to Grow

Copyright © 2025 by Amy Hopkins Gilbride
All rights reserved.

All scriptures taken from the Holy Bible, New King James Version. Copyright ©1982 by Thomas Nelson. Used with permission. All rights reserved

DEDICATIONS

This book is dedicated to you, the reader.
Without you, there would be no purpose for this book.

I also dedicate this book to my family.
I love you forever. You fill my heart with joy.

And mostly, I dedicate this book to the only One who gives us breath and life.
Without Jesus, we would be totally lost.
He is the reason for our entire existence.

PREFACE

Writing a book is not something I ever hoped to do. There are people that dream of writing a book some day; that person was not me. When I was first given the idea and title for this book, I never knew what would become of it. I pondered it in my heart and left it in the back of my mind. It wasn't something I pursued. At times I didn't even know if I would ever complete it.

Then toward the end of 2023, 13 years later, I began to write. It just seemed like the time had finally come. I'm not sure why it took so long to get here, but looking back, I realize that maybe this is the perfect timing after all. Even though there are things that I wish would have never happened, those things have become a part of my story and this book. God used those things to mold me, change me, and bring forth growth. He always has good plans. He can take the ugliest things in this life and bring forth something beautiful.

I am writing this book for you, the reader, hoping that something from my life and my experiences will give you a reason to keep on moving forward. This life can be hard and unfair. It can, at times, be extremely painful. But you are stronger than you know. When you choose to live life past the pain of other's decisions, past what you currently see or currently feel, life takes on a whole new meaning. It is my desire that something you read in this book will give you a more focused reason for living. God is working it out, and it will be good.

TABLE OF CONTENTS

1 Old Heart Made New 1

2 Enlarged Heart 9

3 Medals Are Not for Weak Soldiers 17

4 Take it Out..23

5 Forgiving the Unacceptable 33

6 Wounded Warrior 41

7 You Are Not a Doormat..49

8 More Than Just Right Now......................................53

9 A Speck or a Log 59

10 Restoring What Was Stolen 67

11 Control 75

12 From Death unto Life...85

1
OLD HEART MADE NEW

Deep inside each of us we have a longing, an emptiness that needs to be filled. Our heart longs for more. We are searching and looking for fulfillment. There may be things that our heart gravitates to. We might feel drawn to certain hobbies or have certain interests. We may feel like there must be more to life than we are experiencing. We might even wonder what the purpose of this life is. Sometimes things might seem pointless or meaningless. At other times, we may feel like we have a big heart for certain things that we are passionate about. So many issues or ideas can fill the human heart. But how does God see our heart? What is God's purpose for our heart? What kind of heart does God have, and what kind of heart is He trying to put within us?

Some days might feel like a lot of questions with only a few answers. The truth is, we are not the ones with the answers. We were not made by ourselves or for ourselves. The greater purpose comes from a greater God. So many questions will not be answered until our old heart becomes new. This is where life begins. This is where some of those longings and needs for fulfillment begin to be filled. This is where we really find our true selves. From birth, we all need a new spiritual heart. Born into sin, we all need a Savior.

BORN INTO SIN, WE ALL NEED A SAVIOR

In Ezekiel 36:26-27 it says, "I will give you a new heart and put a new spirit within you; I will take the heart of stone out of your flesh and give you a heart of flesh. I will put My Spirit within you and cause you to walk in My statues, and you will keep My judgments and do them."

God wants to put His Spirit within us. He wants to change us so we will walk in His ways and stay close to His standards. We weren't created to stay the same. This becomes a daily walk that makes us different on the inside, reflecting on the outside. We were created to be different. We were created to get to know Him better and become all that He intended us to be. We were created for a relationship. We were created for eternity.

In John 3, Nicodemus comes to Jesus during the night acknowledging that Jesus is a teacher from God and that God is with Him. Jesus tells Nicodemus that he must be born again. Nicodemus then questions how someone can be born when they are old, or how they can enter into their mother's womb a second time. Jesus then explains that we must be born of water and of the Spirit in order to enter the kingdom of God. There must be a spiritual rebirth. Our old heart must become new. We must be born again. Just as Nicodemus wasn't familiar with this understanding, I do not remember being taught this growing up.

WE MUST BE BORN AGAIN

My brother and I did not have a regular weekly church upbringing - even though our parents did do their best to teach us right from wrong. We were taught good morals and were protected to the best of their knowing. I do remember us being dropped off at Vacation Bible School at times, and we did always say our "God is Great, God is Good" prayer before meals while our momma would say our "Now I Lay Me Down to Sleep" prayer before bed. I also remember our sweet momma reading us Bible stories from a children's Bible book. I always loved those stories. These were good memories for me. At one point, we attempted to start having church in a single-wide trailer on family property. An older minister from Springfield, Louisiana would drive to the trailer in Walker, Louisiana to preach to just a few of us. He was dedicated and faithful. Looking back, I realize how much I loved those meetings. I was always excited when Sunday came, but sadly, it was short lived. I think we may have had church there for about two years. With Brother Matthew's age and declining health, our meetings became less and less until we were no longer able to meet. That trailer sat there for a long time not being used. I do remember playing on the porch and have fond memories of that place. When I got into my teenage years, my childhood best friend, Roxanne, invited me to a Christian concert. It was at a large church in Baton Rouge, Louisiana. I had never experienced anything like that before. I was mesmerized. At the end of that service, they had an altar call for salvation. At that point in my life, I do not remember ever being taught salvation like that. Maybe it was taught at the tiny trailer, but that was the first time I remember hearing it that way. As I saw so many people going down for salvation, I figured I would go too. I liked the thought of Jesus, and something about that service made my heart feel happy, so I went. I filled out a card, but I wouldn't say anything changed in my life. I went on living life just as I had before. Maybe a year or so later, Roxanne had started attending a small church that she invited me to. I decided to go. Toward the end of the service my heart began to pound in my chest as they gave the altar call. I had never experienced that before. I did not really understand what was going on. I felt like I needed to respond, but fear gripped me. I felt like I would almost die if I went and almost die if I didn't. The thoughts of everyone staring at me filled my mind. My feet felt so heavy, so.... I didn't go. That week I thought about what had happened. It wasn't normal for my heart to be racing like that. I didn't say much about it, but I kept wondering what that was and why it happened. Then Roxanne asked me to go back the following Sunday. I decided to go, and lo and behold, the same thing started happening at the time of that altar call. I had a decision to make. All I knew was I had to go, and I had to go NOW! As soon as I made up my mind, I took one step, and then another, and it felt like I was flying down the aisle. My feet were moving fast and with ease. I was taken to the back where a lady sat down with me explaining salvation. I cried and cried. It was different that time. I felt different. To me it was like finding that treasure hidden in the field that the Bible talks about, that pearl of great price. My life changed forever that day on Easter Sunday, April 3, 1994. That day I had found something that I didn't really even know existed. I had always been excited about those childhood Bible stories, but now they were coming alive as I began reading a regular Bible and realizing that those stories weren't just stories. They were real. This is what I needed all along.

Looking back, even though I had said a prayer for salvation at Bethany Church, if I would have died, I don't know if I would have even made it to heaven. It was words spoken from my mouth, but not with a real heart change. I am so thankful that the Lord kept me and protected me while giving me time to truly accept Him. Accepting Jesus is the greatest thing we can ever do. Receiving a new heart is vital in this sin-torn world. But what happens after receiving that new heart? The road of life can get rocky. Life is not always fair, and that new heart can take some beatings. If we are going to walk in the Lord's statues and His ways, we may have to do things a little differently. Our new heart that we received at salvation will still need work. Our way of thinking and doing things will need to change. We are not promised that life here on earth will be all sunshine and roses. There will be trials and tribulations. We will have to walk through things that we didn't expect or even deserve. It all comes down to our heart. God is looking for that old heart to become a new heart that has the ability to be an enlarged heart. Giving Him our heart isn't just a one-time thing. It is a lifetime of learning, growing, and yielding our heart to Him. There will also be times that our born-again heart will need to be enlarged in order to emotionally and mentally get through some things. The same God that saved it is the same God that can enlarge it. One step at a time, He is working it out. Trust the process.

2
ENLARGED HEART

Who would not want their heart enlarged? Now I am not talking about the physical heart. We need that to be its normal size. I am talking about our spiritual heart that needs that Godkind of connection. I remember my MawMaw Eula, my dad's mom, telling me one time that the doctor said she had an enlarged heart. I knew having an enlarged physical heart couldn't be a good thing. Other than that, I had never heard anything about an enlarged heart until the day when I was heading home from my normal weekly visit with my dad in 2010. As far as I remember, it was a good visit. I had no major complaints in my life at that time that I could think of. As I was driving, the Holy Spirit spoke plainly to me, "I'm enlarging your heart." I thought to myself, "Wow! That sounds amazing!" Who wouldn't want an enlarged heart? I knew He was talking about a spiritual heart. I had never given thought to an enlarged spiritual heart before. I was excited. I wanted to always be closer to the Lord, and I wanted to have a heart as big as His or at least as big as it could be.

As I was thinking on what He had said, I instantly had a vision of a big purple heart. The Lord knows that purple is my favorite color, but I knew there was more to it than that. I kept thinking about this and decided to dig deeper. According to Encyclopedia Britannica, the Purple Heart is a U.S. military award that is given to a soldier who is wounded or killed in battle.
i

And according to the Wounded Warrior Regiment Fact Sheet, the following things are listed as wounds/injuries that have historically warranted an award of the Purple Heart:
- Gunshot/ fragmentation wounds
- Lacerations/ fractures
- Perforated eardrum

- Mild traumatic brain injuries /concussions severe enough to cause either loss of consciousness or "not fit for full duty" for a period of more than 48 hours
- Moderate or severe/ penetrating traumatic brain injuries
- Smoke inhalation severe enough to cause 1st to 3rd degree burns to the respiratory tract
- Corneal abrasions
- Effects of chemical, biological or nuclear weapons (to include chlorine gas used in an IED)
- 2nd and 3rd degree burns.[ii]

That was a whole lot to think about. What seemed so exciting was becoming more real. Wounded, killed, or injured does not sound extremely exciting. To think of the things that soldiers have to physically go through in order to receive a Purple Heart medal does not sound that wonderful at all. It actually sounds quite awful. I was not so sure that I liked the thought of having an enlarged, purple heart after all. Soldiers give their lives to serve and protect people who would not even do the same for them, and some of those people would even turn their backs on them. They sacrifice for people that only think of themselves all while putting their own lives in vulnerable, life-threatening situations. Living a life of sacrifice and putting others above ourselves isn't normally something we would choose, but it does sound a lot like Jesus.

Shortly after this, the idea of God enlarging my heart took on a whole new meaning. My excitement faded when I realized that having an enlarged heart would take sacrifice on my part, and there would be a price to pay.

There are times when we must learn to push past our own pain, disappointment, discouragement, and frustration while we think of the greater picture. Our heart must enlarge to take on things we would never have expected. Some things are simply wrong, but we must continue moving forward.

> OUR HEART MUST ENLARGE TO TAKE ON THINGS WE WOULD NEVER HAVE EXPECTED

Papa G, who has been a spiritual father to us, has made this wise and true statement, "Sometimes we are bleeding, while we are leading." We will all face situations that cause us to bleed. There will be painful situations that our hearts just can't handle, but in all of that, we must keep going. Through it all, our decisions and how we handle things can affect more than just us. Even though we may be bleeding on the inside, there are people watching us, looking up to us, and needing us to keep on leading. A true soldier has to keep leading even while bleeding. We will need a greater love, a set mind, and a heart of determination. These things will cause our heart to be enlarged.

Shortly after the Lord had given me the vision of the purple heart, our oldest daughter, Kailee, fourteen years old at the time, surprised me with a gift she had made. It was a small black clay swan. In the center of it was a purple heart. I don't think she understood the significance of it at that time, but it definitely touched my heart. The timing was perfect. I knew that only the Lord could have given her that idea. Of all of the things she could have made and all of the colors that she could have used, she chose a black swan with a purple heart. The purple heart was obvious to me at that point. I wasn't extremely sure about the black swan. I do remember looking it up at that time with no understanding, but in a recent Google search, I read the definition of a black swan as an occurrence or phenomenon that comes as a surprise because it was not predicted or was hard to predict.[iii] Wikipedia gives this definition of the black swan theory: an event that comes as a surprise, has a major effect, and is often inappropriately rationalized after the fact with the benefit of hindsight. [iv]

Looking back now, it makes perfect sense. Have you ever had a situation that seemed to come out of nowhere? Something that seemed so unexpected? Something that could be so negatively life changing? Some unexpected, life situations come as a shock and can leave us with feelings of trauma. They can leave us in a dark place of despair that seems like there is no way out. If situations were always known before, it may be easier to deal with, but when it is unforeseen, that shock can feel like our world is completely, permanently shaken.

There will be times in life that you just don't know how to get through. You can't just wish it away. You can't just ignore it. You can't do it alone. These types of situations are just, no way around it, hard. Some things do not just clear up fast. A quick prayer just doesn't fix it. They say that time heals all wounds. As time passes, things do sometimes get easier, but it can take a lot of time for that to happen. Time can be a blessing and a curse. When you are waiting for that time to get here, it can seem like it is never coming. I always say, "One day at a time." Take it one day at a time. We aren't meant to handle more than that. The Bible tells us not to worry about tomorrow. Tomorrow will have its own troubles. Live for today. Tomorrow isn't here and yesterday is gone. Some days are better than others, but you can still make the best out of every day. We must live right now while we have life. Now is the time. Make something good out of your day. Make something good out of your life. Hold on, it might seem rough at times, but when God enlarges your heart, you will come through as a survivor. You might be bleeding but keep on leading. Your heart is being enlarged.

3
MEDALS ARE NOT FOR WEAK SOLDIERS

2 Timothy 2:3-4, "You therefore must endure hardship as a good soldier of Jesus Christ. No one engaged in warfare entangles himself with the affairs of this life, that he may please Him who enlisted him as a soldier."

Imagine being in a battle and those that are defending you are just sitting around eating potato chips and watching Netflix. Not that there is anything extremely wrong with eating some potato chips or taking some down time, but would you feel secure and protected by this kind of soldier? Imagine a soldier that gets so caught up in drama or the things of this world that he gets sidetracked from his assignment. The battle is taking place, but the soldier isn't actively participating. If a soldier is consumed by unnecessary things, how can he be effective?

Whether we realize it or not, there is a battle raging. We are at war with an invisible enemy that shows up visible through pain, heartache, and troubles. This enemy seeks to kill, steal, and destroy. From the time we are born until the time we exit this earth; we will be in a battle. Prayerfully, most days there will not be active war; but nevertheless, there will be a battle going on.

Each of us have been positioned on this earth for this time, for this place, and for this season. We can wreak havoc, or we can repair the breaches. We can be a part of the problem or an answer to the solution. There is an invading army, and we must decide whose side we are on.

A soldier that sees the battle coming and retreats is not much of a soldier. A soldier that cowers down will be defeated, and not only will he be defeated, but all of those that he is sent to protect will be injured or defeated as well. As Christians, we are called to be soldiers. We are not called to be cowardly or unbelieving. We are called to face the battle.

Revelation 21:8 tells us, "But the cowardly, unbelieving, abominable, murderers, sexually immoral, sorcerers, idolaters, and all liars shall have their part in the lake which burns with fire and brimstone, which is the second death."

As Christians, we often see a problem with murder, sexual immorality, witchcraft, sorcery, and lying, but often do not think as much about being fearful, cowardly, or unbelieving. We tend to be more lenient on fear and cowardness, but more dogmatic on other issues. So, what exactly is a coward? According to Dictionary.com, "a coward is a person who lacks courage in facing danger, opposition, pain, etc., a timid or easily intimidated person.[v]

No one wants to experience dangerous, painful, or unpleasant things, which is understandable, but a true soldier needs to face the battle. A true soldier must not entangle himself with the affairs of this life. A true soldier does not cower to or accept defeat. We have been enlisted by the ultimate soldier, Jesus Christ, Himself. When faced with the most horrible, gruesome death, Jesus chose courage. When ridiculed, tortured, and betrayed, He chose bravery over fear. He did not run from it but chose to face it. In His pain, He saw the bigger picture. He saw redemption. Maybe in your own pain, you only see the pain. It might be hard to deal with, and to deny its existence would be easy. I get it. I really do. I feel your pain. My pain might be different from your pain, but pain is pain and is never pleasant. Walking away or retreating might seem easier, but will that bring true victory? Ignoring the pain will not make it just disappear. The enemy would love for you to lay down and die in your own misery and defeat. He wants us to wallow in our own self-pity. He would love to keep us so focused on our circumstances that there seems to be no hope left. Not to make light of your circumstances but staying there is not going to change anything. Staying there will not get you out of that deep pit that you are in. It will only prolong the process of healing that needs to take place. This is why our focus has to change. We will become what we gaze at. The longer the gaze in the wrong direction, the longer the defeat.

2 Corinthians 4:17-18 says:

"For our light affliction, which is but for a moment, is working for us a far more exceeding and eternal weight of glory, while we do not look at the things which are seen, but at the things which are not seen. For the things which are seen are temporary, but the things which are not seen are eternal."

WE WILL BECOME WHAT WE GAZE AT

Though things can be painful and may seem to last forever, in comparison to eternity, our afflictions are for a moment. As we face life's troubles, our focus must not be on what we see with our natural eyes, but on the eternal things that we cannot yet see. God has a way of turning things around. He has a way of making things wonderful again. Your pain might just have a purpose. What is so painful now could be preparing you for greater glory to come. When the enemy thinks he has won, remember that Jesus is not finished yet. Pick up your sword, take hold of your spiritual weapons, and fight. Refuse to retreat. Boldly face your fears. Be the soldier that you were called to be. This season will not last forever. Remember that your strength comes from the Lord. You are not alone and cannot expect to do it on your own. The Holy Spirit is there to battle with you to keep moving you forward. Even though it might come with a price, your reward is waiting for you. A medal of honor will be given to those who overcome. In your own strength you may fail, but in His strength, you are more than a conqueror. Jesus loves you! He sees all and knows all. He has seen the battle. He understands the pain and the struggle. His heart breaks for you, and His blood was shed to heal you. Take a deep breath and press on. Medals are not awarded to weak soldiers, and you, my friend, are stronger than you think.

4
TAKE IT OUT

Sometimes life throws us cruel blows. We can do everything that we know to do that is right, minding our own business, living the best life that we can when suddenly something happens that we never expected. We may be living a peaceful life when someone else's wrong decisions wreck our world. There can be times that test our faith and seek to destroy our soul. Can you think of something like this in your own life? Was there a day when things became too much? Was there a time when you didn't know how you would be able to continue on? Even through much prayer, you weren't sure how you would survive?

No one wants to experience life's hard lessons, but some things are out of our control. So, what are we to do? How are we to handle these devastations? When these things happen, we tend to emotionally really take them in. They invade our thinking and cause us to rehash the trauma of it all. It can fester and cause infection. What we allow to be taken in can affect what comes out. These things can only be handled by God enlarging our hearts. Our own frail, fragile hearts can only handle so much. I'm sure you have heard the saying, "Garbage in, garbage out." When garbage or wrong thinking is taken in, we can't expect good things to come out. We have a responsibility to do something about it. Usually when the trash gets full, we take it out but imagine if we never took it out. Imagine the stench. It would be a rotten, smelly mess. The smell would become horrendous. Can you imagine our own heart smelling like this? We could try justifying it by saying that we are not the ones that put the trash in there in the first place, that it wasn't our place to take it out, or that it was someone else's fault that it had become a smelly mess. The truth is, we are responsible for our own heart regardless of how the trash got put in there in the first place. Ouch! I know that it isn't pleasing to our ears and not easy on our heart.

Trash is not made to stay inside. Whether it is our own trash or someone else's, there is a proper way to dispose of it. Many times, we are not in control of what happens to us, but we are in control of how we handle what happens to us. This can be very difficult. No lie! We tend to take in what needs to be left out. The pain, hurt, betrayal, rejection, disappointment, frustrations... you name it, they all try to become a part of us. They want to latch on like leaches that suck the very life out of us. We might feel like we have no control over the pain that devastation has caused. Many times, we can nurse old wounds and hold on to them as if they are our friends. This is all part of the enemy's plan to keep us trapped in that time, instead of us moving forward. Wounds often cause walls to go up. It becomes a protective mechanism, but when we rehash things repeatedly it only causes us more pain. It's like leaving the garbage inside to only fester, rot, and stink even more. Who wants to smell stinky, vile garbage? It all goes back to not allowing the evil that others do to us to become a part of who we should be. If hate and bitterness become a part of our own heart, we are becoming a part of evil ourselves. Our own heart can begin to smell like the garbage that we never put in to begin with. Some things are made to be taken out and not left in.

Ephesians 4:26-27:
"Be angry, and do not sin; do not let the sun go down on your wrath, nor give place to the devil."

God is angry with wickedness. Injustices done to us or others do not go unnoticed by Him. It might seem like people just get away with things, but they do not. Sadly, the evil they allow will bring destruction to their own lives. When we understand the principles of God, we become like Jesus and say, "Father forgive them, for they do not know what they do." This has to be the only option. If we really comprehend the full picture of our decisions, we would all live differently. Jesus died for so much more.

The anger we feel, although justified, is not meant to be carried. There will be times when we have to work through these feelings, but we cannot stay in that place. Be angry, but do not stay angry. Each night, give it to God, go to sleep, and get some rest. If those feelings are creeping in the next day, give it to God again. Cast your cares on Him because He does care about you. He can handle it. Express the pain and hurt, cry out to Him, and ask Him for help. Plead with Him if you must. Pray that the pain will not attach to you. These things aren't made to be taken in. They are made to be taken out.

As I am speaking to you, I am speaking from some experience. There have been times in my life that I could have allowed the garbage to stay in. I could have allowed bitterness to grow. I could have chosen to live in the past, and to hold on to the things that have caused me pain. I wouldn't say that I have handled things completely right every time. Sometimes I probably failed miserably. We are all learning and growing as we go. When we go through things that we have never been through before, we must walk it out as we go. The process can be painful. Let me tell you, it isn't easy, but it is possible.

One of these situations happened in my life in 2005. My husband, our two daughters, and I were heading to church. A vehicle came toward us in our lane. My husband pulled the wheel to avoid a head on collision, but the oncoming vehicle came toward us a second time. It honestly seemed almost deliberate. I remember bracing myself and saying, "Oh, God!" I blacked out upon impact. Our vehicle went off the road, through a ditch, and hit a tree. I remember my husband coming to my side of the vehicle and telling me to get out. Somehow, I knew that I couldn't move, and I told him that I couldn't. The airbags had gone off, and it seemed smokey in the vehicle. It surely wasn't the best day of my life. The ambulance workers loaded our daughters and me into the ambulance. The ride seemed to last forever. I remember quietly praying aloud in the ambulance. I mostly prayed in tongues. I'm sure the ambulance workers thought I had lost my mind, but the Holy Spirit was keeping me sane that day. My ankle was so swollen that my jeans, my favorite jeans, had to be cut off. After what seemed like forever, I was told that I would be taken into emergency surgery. I wasn't ready for this. I just wanted to go home. This was not on my list of things to do for the day for sure!

I remember waking up from surgery and seeing the surgeon, my husband, and my dad standing at the foot of the bed. I later remembered seeing a man with brownish hair in a white suit sitting beside the bed during surgery. I believe that this was an angel that was sent to be with me during this difficult time. I am extremely grateful for everyone and everything that got me through that time.

This was one of those situations that did not go away so easily. An external fixture was placed through my right leg and my ankle. This was to stay in place until permanent hardware could be put in. The surgeon said that my ankle injury was one of the worst he had seen. He also stated that when he cut it open for surgery, there were five pieces of bone just floating around in there. This was one of those life-changing situations that would have to be walked out, literally, as I went but the Lord has been faithful. Life-changing situations have a way of teaching us a lot of lessons. Some of the things that I figured out during that time are:

- How to mop in a wheelchair
- How to cook standing up on one leg
- How to drive with my left foot
- How to ride a bicycle with a walking boot on
- How to hop on one foot while loading groceries to the conveyor belt
- How to take "bird baths" in the shower

It made life interesting for sure. Everything had to be done more carefully. Looking back now, I'm sure some of this looked comical, but I was determined to make the best out of it. I did my best to focus on the good that I still had and not on the pain. A lot of things in life are about perspective. How we see things affects many outcomes. I was thankful to still be alive. I was thankful to have one good leg and two functioning arms. I was thankful that with surgery I could have the ability to walk again. I was thankful that even though I was in the wheelchair for a few months, spiritually I wasn't bound. Things weren't like I wanted them, but I was thankful. And more than anything, I was thankful that I was able to forgive.

As many of you probably already know, life isn't always easy. There are challenges and obstacles. Sometimes it is very painful, but we can do our best to see some good out of all the bad. We can do our best to be a better person when others are not. It's so important to keep our own heart right when things aren't right. We can't do anything on our own, but the good news is that the Holy Spirit is there as our comforter and helper. More than anything else, I learned to trust God. We can do all things through Christ that gives us strength.

Shortly after the accident, we were hit with another blow. The oncoming driver tried to sue us. We were already told that he had a history of accidents and suing people. Sure enough, this was the case.

The day of the accident, he and his passenger walked away from the accident while our daughters and I were taken by ambulance. Our youngest daughter had a fractured jaw. Thankfully, she only had to eat soft food for a while and no surgery was required. I know it could have been so much worse!

We found out later that the driver was an excluded driver from his daughter's policy, and he was driving her vehicle. He was ticketed on the day of the accident. The day of the court proceeding, I was at home in the wheelchair while my husband attended. The driver of the oncoming vehicle somehow had "witnesses" show up. On the day of the accident, we never saw any of these witnesses there. He managed to get his ticket dropped. The passenger of his vehicle was awarded ten thousand dollars from our insurance company. The driver, being an unauthorized driver, was not insured. None of my medical bills were covered by the other vehicles insurance. I knew it was very important to keep my own heart right. Even though I knew that this accident was a huge injustice, it was very important for myself and my family to forgive quickly. I could not allow what had happened to us to become a part of us. Many things in life are tests. How we handle these things has a huge weight in Heaven. We are being watched and cheered on. So much of this life will determine the life we live after this. We are called to live it well.

A lot of what happens to us or others around us can affect us greatly. We tend to take things to heart. We feel those things. We live those things. We experience those things. Our feelings are very real and do not need to be dismissed, but they do need to be worked through. Hopefully one day we will look back with thankfulness at what we survived. In our feelings and in our living, we are still only responsible for what we allow to come in and what we decide to take out. Some things aren't even worth taking in. The longer the trash stays, the smellier it gets. Do yourself a favor and take it out.

5
FORGIVING THE UNACCEPTABLE

Being a Christian is probably one of the hardest things we can be called to do. As a Christian, we are called to a higher standard. We can no longer live however we want. We are not our own. If we plan to follow Jesus, we are called to walk how He walked. Let me tell you, that is some huge shoes to fill. I sit back sometimes and think, "How did He possibly do it!?" It blows my mind. I know it was His dependency on His Heavenly Father, but even still, that can seem like a far-off task. Compared to others, we might think we are doing well, but compared to Jesus' standard, we miss the mark. We are all a work in progress, and thankfully, He has given us this time in life to get it right.

One of the hardest things sometimes, as Christians, is to forgive. Sure, we like to be forgiven ourselves but lending that forgiveness can be very difficult. Peter asked the Lord how many times he had to forgive someone that sinned against him. Seven times? Apparently, Peter thought seven times should be sufficient. Think about that. If someone does something against us once, although maybe wrong, we can kind of overlook it. Everyone makes mistakes. The second time we figure that they should have learned the first time, but we might be willing to give them another chance. Depending on the severity of it, the third time really starts pushing it. How could they not learn? Peter's seven times seems more than reasonable to me. What about you? What do you think? I'm sure Peter even thought he was being reasonable. Jesus lets Peter know that seven times isn't enough. What!? Doesn't that seem kind of harsh to the person that is being sinned against? If a person has sinned against us, do we need to forgive them over and over again? There are some things that are hard to wrap our mind around. But Jesus knows our frailty. He knows that sometimes people do wrong things. He knows that sometimes we ourselves do wrong things too. He also knows that sometimes people do the right things, but for wrong reasons. Even the right things done for wrong reasons can be wrong. And knowing the right thing to do, but not doing it is also wrong and considered sinful. It can get complicated. Jesus is looking for changed hearts, obedient hearts, and hearts with pure motives. That new heart that we receive at salvation is being worked on. Keeping that heart pure will definitely require some continued work. Each individual heart is Jesus' goal. He's got a lot of work to oversee.

We are called to forgive to keep our own heart clean, but what about unacceptable behavior? Just because we are called to forgive doesn't mean we have to accept any type of behavior. I have heard many sermons on forgiveness. They tend to be geared toward those that have messed up and made wrong decisions. There is no doubt that God is a forgiving God to those with a repentant heart. I thank the Lord for His forgiveness. I thank Him that He is merciful. We are all in need of forgiveness and mercy at times. I understand these truths and concepts. The problem I have isn't with messages of God's forgiveness. The problem is that these messages can leave those that have been hurt and sinned against feeling as if the things done against them should be no big deal. Just "forgive and move on" so to speak. These messages can make those that have sinned against others just accept that they are forgiven while making light of their mistakes. These messages can cause those that are sinning against others to not see the true consequences of their actions. There needs to be true repentance, a true change of heart and a turning in thinking. There needs to be a change of heart so there is a change of action. The message of forgiveness is not a license to continue messing up. If the consequences were better understood, the sin might be cut off. I have heard that other countries are less tolerant of wrongdoings. If a thief is caught in some countries, a person's fingers or hand is cut off. Although a little extreme, I'm sure that would make a person think before stealing. We have a couple of references in the Bible regarding this same concept. In Matthew 5:27-30 it says:

"You have heard that it was said to those of old, 'You shall not commit adultery.' But I say to you that whoever looks at a woman to lust for her has already committed adultery with her in his heart. If your right eye causes you to sin, pluck it out and cast *it* from you; for it is more profitable for you that one of your members perish, than for your whole body to be cast into hell. And if your right hand causes you to sin, cut it off and cast *it* from you; for it is more profitable for you that one of your members perish, than for your whole body to be cast into hell."

Then in Matthew 18:8-9 it says:

"If your hand or foot causes you to sin, cut it off and cast *it* from you. It is better for you to enter into life lame or maimed, rather than having two hands or two feet, to be cast into the everlasting fire. And if your eye causes you to sin, pluck it out and cast *it* from you. It is better for you to enter into life with one eye, rather than having two eyes, to be cast into hell fire."

I do not believe that these scriptures are meant to be taken literally. We do not need to be going around plucking out eyes or cutting off body parts. This is meant as good advice and a warning about the seriousness that needs to be taken to make sure we cut off things from our lives that could destroy us or destroy others. It is better to cut off one part of the body instead of the entire body being cast into hell. For the person that needs forgiveness, a sermon about their sin being forgiven, it being cast as far as the east is from the west, and God remembering it no more sounds wonderful, but for the person sinned against, this can be painful. The person that committed the wrong has become the injured one while the person that is wronged is just expected to get over it.

When David committed sin with Bathsheba, there were consequences. David suffered heartache and the loss of his child due to his sin. His sin wasn't just forgiven as if nothing had happened. In his forgiveness, there was still suffering. The damage he had done was done. He couldn't undo it. He needed forgiveness, at the same time, what about the pain of Uriah's family? Not only had David committed adultery with Uriah's wife, but he also saw to it that Uriah was killed in battle to cover up David's own sin. Uriah was a son to someone, maybe a father, brother or friend to others. What about the pain of their loss? They each had to go through their own pain because of David's selfish decisions against an innocent man. David was supposed to be a man after God's own heart, but this wasn't the heart of God. God's heart is always to the brokenhearted. He comes to bind up their wounds. He leans in toward the most innocent. He is angry with wickedness. It is often said, "Hurt people, hurt people." This is a true statement. People need healing, so they do not continue to hurt others. We, ourselves, included. Our messages need to get to the root so that healing takes place. The world needs healed people that heal people. The church needs messages that help people become overcomers. It needs real, raw truth that pulls people out of the lowest pit so that mistakes aren't continued. Our decisions have an effect on others – even if we are forgiven. We each have our own will, but that will can cause others pain. We must take ownership of our faults. Sin needs to be dealt with and not just covered up. If someone sins against us, we can't allow the pain we've experienced to destroy us. That pain needs to be dealt with properly. Even though we have been wronged, legitimately, we can become like the ones that hurt us if we do not guard our own heart. This is where an enlarged heart comes in. We need to understand that there are inherited weaknesses that need to be eradicated. Soul ties need to be broken. Demonic forces need to be confronted, and flesh needs to be crucified. Many people do not want to admit their weaknesses. So many things are kept in the darkness, and this is where the enemy works best. When darkness is exposed, the light shines on the situation. The enemy begins to lose his power when the truth is revealed. It is understandable that people often keep silent about their troubles because of fear of embarrassment or fear of how they will be looked at and treated afterwards. Pride often keeps them from getting the help that they need. This is all part of the enemy's plan to keep people from escaping his grip. The more sin is hidden, the more it grows. When the light shines on it, it begins to diminish. There needs to be more accountability. When a person can truly repent and turn away from their destructive behavior, healing can come. Without repentance, any accepted behavior will likely continue. We are called to forgive unacceptable behavior, but we are not called to accept unacceptable behavior. Sometimes a line must be drawn, a standard must be raised, and consequences need to be laid out. To keep our own heart right, sometimes we need those boundaries. We can protect the heart that God has given us without having walls of unforgiveness and bitterness surround us. Wisdom is needed. We sometimes need a strategic plan and determination to carry out that plan. Part of being a soldier is standing our ground and refusing to let the enemy have his way. This sometimes requires confrontation, boldness, and a refusal to back down. We might be called to forgive the unacceptable but remember that we do not have to accept the unacceptable. Forgive, but do not accept the unacceptable.

6
WOUNDED WARRIOR

We are called to forgive, but refusing to remember what has been done to us can be a tiring process. The enemy will gladly send fiery arrows into our mind causing us to remember. A wounded soul can cause our thinking to be triggered. It can associate certain things of the past with current situations -even if those current situations are different this time. The brain is a powerful organ of our body, but when our soul is emotionally injured it can cause a lot of unnecessary pain. Healing needs to take place. Negative thoughts need to be cast down. Each time we remember, we need to forgive again. Even though we forgive with our will, the pain can still be there. Even though we choose to show love, the hurt can still feel very real. Those that have somehow been wounded in life have a choice to give in to defeat or choose to do something with what is left. A wounded warrior's life will not be the same, but it can still be of great value. Things might need to be done differently, but there is still a purpose. Life can be lived again.

3 John 2
"Beloved, I pray that you may prosper in all things and be in health, just as your soul prospers."

This is a powerful scripture. I remember one Sunday, after my car accident, being at church and looking around the room. At this time, I was in my wheelchair. The worship was really amazing that day. My heart so wanted to be out of that wheelchair so I could really worship the Lord like I felt He deserved, but here I was confined to the chair. My body was confined, but my heart and spirit were free. As I looked around, some people sat down, and others just stood there without raising their hands. I realize that different people express themselves differently during worship and there was no judgment on my part, but as I scanned the room the Lord spoke to me that there were people in that room that were more crippled than

I was. Even though they had two good functioning legs, they were bound. They weren't truly free. At that moment I was sad for them but also filled with gratitude. I would have much rather been in that wheelchair while free in my mind than to have had two functioning legs yet crippled in my thinking. I knew at that moment that my soul was prospering. My body might have needed time to heal, but it was well with my soul. I made up my mind that if or when I got out of that wheelchair, I wouldn't be just sitting around withholding my praise when the King was passing by. The Lord wants us to prosper in all things and be in health just as our soul prospers. Is your soul prospering? Is your mind free and at peace? A physical wound can last a lifetime. We can live a long time with a physical injury yet still be free in our mind. A wounded warrior doesn't have to stay wounded. Wounds can be healed. There can be things that seem like they will never go away and feelings that follow us everywhere. If we are not careful, these feelings can begin to show up in our body. I might not completely understand it, but I do know that emotions that are not dealt with can make us physically sick. I do believe that many physical sicknesses have a spiritual root. We can pray all day, for months, or even for years without any relief at times until we get to the root. Don't forget that the enemy is good at hiding. If he can keep himself hidden, he can continue to work. It is our job to find him out, resist him, and get him to running. It does us no justice to hold on to hurts, traumas, or fears. We need to be quick to release things. There are things in life that can cause Post Traumatic Stress Disorder. PTSD is a real thing. Things that happen to us have the ability to rule over us. If our soul is going to prosper, we must deal with those things.

    Here in Louisiana, we aren't strangers to hurricanes. In August of 2021, hurricane Ida hit. This storm personally hit us differently than other hurricanes. I believe it was around 8:00 p.m. when a large oak tree from our front yard fell through our house. The sound was loud, the wind was whipping through, and the water was pouring in. I would say it was a traumatic event. Throughout the night, Robert, Jena, our daughter; Camilla, our dog; and myself kept hearing the sounds of the wind along with loud booming sounds. We didn't sleep at all, not even for a few minutes. Needless to say, it was a very long night. As daylight broke, we realized that the booming sounds we had heard were the trees falling, all around us. It looked like a warzone. Even though it was an awful sight, I can't tell you how grateful I was for the storm to be over, for the sun to be shining, and that we had all survived. There was so much loss and so much to be done, but it was a good day to be alive. This is how life is at times, the storm comes, the storm passes through, but we survive - even with much loss, the sun begins to shine again.

    We are not exempt from troubles in this life. We never know what we might have to deal with, but wounded warriors keep moving forward. You might need the help of someone to get you to a better place, but stopping isn't an option. Until we take our last breath on this earth, we have to keep breathing and believing. Sometimes, it might feel like the pain will last forever. There might need to be some repairs or complete rebuilding, but when you seek the Healer, you will come to a day when you realize what bothered you before doesn't bother you anymore. It's like something was attached to you and it just fell off. Somewhere along the way, it was no longer there. To no longer be weighed down with those burdens is the greatest feeling. Remember that you might be bleeding while you're leading for a while, but there comes a time when the bleeding stops. Think about a physical wound for a minute. A fresh wound might bleed and bleed some more. Pressure will need to be applied to get the bleeding to finally stop. Once the bleeding is under control, the wound still takes some time to heal. The pain might linger for quite a while. Redness and bruising might be a part of the process. The wound will begin to crust over as a protective mechanism. We can see how a physical wound is healed with time and process, just as an emotional wound can take time and process. The healing doesn't always happen overnight. If we continue to pick at the wound, the wound isn't likely to heal. Infection is also likely to set in. The wound needs to be cleaned and covered. If we are ever to get past an emotional wound, there has to be a cleansing of our emotions while spending more time thinking about good things. We must learn to not continue picking at those wounds and to instead cover those in prayer.

One of the strangest visions I have had recently was of Jesus licking a wound on His arm. It was very bizarre to me, but as I thought about this, I heard the Holy Spirit say, "Sometimes you have to lick your wounds and move on." Although strange, I knew the Lord was conveying a message to me through that vision. Even in nature, animals lick their wounds. This is done as a way of not only cleaning and soothing themselves, but it also helps with the pain, antibacterial properties, and blood clotting. We might need to tend to our wounds, but we do what we need to do, and we move on. If anyone understands wounds, Jesus does. If anyone understands healing, Jesus does. We don't have time to waste. We don't have time to stay stuck in a place of pain and loss. Even though it might take some time to heal, that time needs to be used on healing and not on reinfecting. My momma used to say, "You can't cry over spilled milk." If the milk has spilled, there's not much you can do about it but clean it up. What is done is done. Start the process of healing. Work on cleaning up the mess. A warrior gets wounds, but they lick their wounds and continue on. Wounds do not disqualify a true warrior. A true warrior might be a wounded warrior, but they are a winning warrior as they continue on. Keep winning wounded warrior. It might be difficult, but you are not finished yet.

7
YOU ARE NOT A DOORMAT

In Christianity, you might feel like you are required to be a doormat. Accept the beating, so to speak. Just deal with the disgrace and be willing to put up with whatever comes your way. Aren't we called to turn the other cheek? Remember, the truth is that Jesus is after our heart. He doesn't want the evil we see in others to become evil in us. Turning the other cheek has more to do with what we allow in our own heart.

Romans 12:21:
"Do not be overcome by evil but overcome evil with good."

Jesus does not want us to be overcome by evil. Choosing evil only creates more evil. We overcome evil with the opposite of evil. We overcome evil by doing good. Jesus said that the enemy had no place in Him. He gave no place to the devil. He chose His battles wisely, and He leaned on the Holy Spirit. When the Bible says that we do not fight against flesh and blood, it isn't just some nice sounding cliché. We truly are not fighting against people. That always needs to be at the forefront of our mind. This is how Jesus was able to forgive because He knew they truly didn't comprehend what they were doing. Jesus understood who He was really at war with. He understood the great deception and where that came from. When we separate the person from the evil we see, we realize that the person has only become a puppet in the hands of an evil master. Something has entered their heart that contradicts the heart of the Savior. Sometimes good people do bad things. Sometimes people allow the evil of the enemy to dominate their heart. They accept the lie instead of the complete truth and gravitate toward what pleases the flesh, all while the delusion of the

> **THE DELUSION OF THE ENEMY CAUSES A LACK OF RESTRAINT**

enemy causes a lack of restraint. A perfect plan of the enemy.

John 8:44 says, "You are of your father the devil, and the desires of your father you want to do. He was a murderer from the beginning, and does not stand in the truth, because there is no truth in him. When he speaks a lie, he speaks from his own resources, for he is liar and the father of it."

Jesus says you are of your father the devil.... Who is our father? What attributes are we following? The devil is the father of murder, lies, lust, deception, and every form of evil we can think of. Those that follow him show evidence of it.

1 John 3:7-8 says, "Little children, let no one deceive you. He who practices righteousness is righteous, just as He is righteous. He who sins is of the devil, for the devil has sinned from the beginning. For this purpose, the Son of God was manifested, that He might destroy the works of the devil."

The human nature that we were born into has a desire for sin. Desires of the flesh can at times seem greater than the will of our spirit. If we are wronged, our flesh seeks retaliation. If we are hurt, our flesh wants the person to suffer. In 1 Peter 3:9, we are told to not return evil for evil or reviling for reviling. Also, in Romans 12 it talks about not repaying evil for evil but doing our best to live peacefully with others while leaving vengeance to the Lord. We must work out our own salvation with fear and trembling and allow the Lord to work on others. We do not need to allow the evil of the enemy or the evil we see functioning in others to control us. We are called to practice righteousness. Jesus came to destroy the works of the devil, not participate with it.

Protect your own heart from the entrance of evil. Give no place to the devil. Do not let the evil you see in others become evil inside of you.

Living as a Christian might feel like you are being a doormat. You are not a doormat. When we refuse to retaliate or gain revenge, we are following the example of our Father in Heaven.

8
MORE THAN JUST RIGHT NOW

As believers, we are called to live for more than just the here and now. Life has a way of consuming our time. The enemy sends distractions and roadblocks. If we are not careful, we can get trapped in former periods of time when life was better or paralyzed by the painful events of the past. The enemy might not prevent us from being saved or from entering Heaven, but he will do everything he can to prevent us from being all that we can be for God's kingdom. The enemy plans to keep us captive. That's the enemy's plan. To keep us there. The Lord has different plans. He wants the captives set free, truly free.

In Jeremiah 29, Jeremiah writes a letter to the captives who Nebuchadnezzar had taken captive from Jerusalem to Babylon. It tells us that the Lord caused them to be carried away as captives. This wasn't some cruel thing from the Lord. It was a result of their sin and disobedience. Their own sin and disobedience already held them captive. The Lord wanted them to be free from that. His goal was for them to turn to Him with all their heart, but this wasn't something that they were willingly doing on their own.

Jeremiah 29:11
"For I know the thoughts that I think toward you, says the Lord, thoughts of peace and not of evil, to give you a future and a hope."

The Lord had a plan for them to prosper, not to harm them, and planned to give them hope and a future. That hasn't changed today. God still has good plans for us. He has good plans even for those that sin against us. The Lord never takes pleasure in people getting away from the truth. He doesn't take pleasure in evil or wickedness. But He does take pleasure in people returning to Him. We can all be like sheep that have gone astray and turned to our own way. It can be easy to want our own way. God's ways are higher than our ways. Some things are above our comprehension. The sad truth is, sometimes people will not return to God until things get bad. It sometimes takes rough circumstances to produce life giving results. What can seem so tragic in this life could be the very thing that turns things around.

Let's look at the story of Joseph in Genesis 37. Joseph loved God. He was excited about all that God was showing him, but I don't think that Joseph thought it would all happen the way it did. He probably never expected to have to go through everything he went through. I'm sure when Joseph was dreaming, he wouldn't have realized that his brothers were scheming. We must realize that not everyone will be happy for us when God does things in our lives. When we are blessed, some people will get angry about it. People can start having ill feelings against us when we have not even done anything to them. Envy and jealousy can begin to eat away at them. Envy and jealousy are horrible attributes to have. A person that is envious or jealous of others will do whatever they need to do to discredit or get rid of someone else. Spirits

> I'M SURE WHEN JOSEPH WAS DREAMING, HE WOULDN'T HAVE REALIZED THAT HIS BROTHERS WERE SCHEMING

of envy and jealousy often become murderous against others for no real reason. It eats away at their soul and torments their mind. It causes the smallest thing to become something far greater than it is. It causes the mind to justify its thinking. None of us need to give room to these things.

James 3:14-16 says,
"But if you have bitter envy and self-seeking in your hearts, do not boast and lie against the truth. This wisdom does not descend from above, but is earthly, sensual, demonic. For where envy and self-seeking exist, confusion and every evil thing are there."

If we feel even an ounce of envy, jealousy or self-seeking in our heart, we need to cut it off and refuse to give it access. We must treat the things that are contrary to God as the enemy that they are. Amid confusion, there will be envy and self-seeking. We should not be seeking for self but seeking for the kingdom of God and the good of others. If you find these things in your heart, do not cover it up. Do not pretend or deny the truth. Deal with it and get rid of it.

I'm sure Joseph didn't realize how much his own heart would have to enlarge to take him where his dream was going. And I'm sure it must have been painful for him for his own brothers to not only not share in his joy, but to be angry and envious about it.

The promise can seem beautiful until the process is revealed. If you've ever waited for a promise, you probably know that there is often pain in that waiting time. Joseph endured much hardship, but he ended up coming out on top. I believe the way he handled the situations handed to him had a lot to do with his victorious end. Joseph could have been held captive by bitterness, resentment, and unforgiveness if he had not chosen to forgive. The enemy had set it up for his destruction, but Joseph passed his test. He went on with his life and continued to be blessed. He obviously trusted the Lord.

In Genesis 50:20, we read that Joseph tells his brothers:
"But as for you, you meant evil against me; but God meant it for good, in order to bring it about as it is this day, to save many people alive."

Through everything that Joseph had to go through, God was orchestrating good. God's plan was bigger than just Joseph, and if I had to guess, I would say that God's plan is bigger than just you and me. As you trust Him, He is working all things out for your good. It might be painful, and it might not be easy, but it will work out for good.

This life is more than just here and now. There is a greater picture. There is a greater plan. We do not have control over everyone else. We are only responsible for ourselves, and that is a big enough job of its own. Guard your own heart and focus on something greater than what you see right now, because we are living for more than just right now.

9
A SPECK OR A LOG

How many times have you heard someone say, "Don't judge me" or "No one can judge me" or "Only God can judge me." These are common phrases for those that just don't want to hear it. The truth is, sometimes things need to be addressed. If a person is living outside of God's boundaries, we can expect that it will not work out well for them. Boundaries are set in place for a reason. These are for everyone's safety and protection, even though sometimes people feel like no one should tell them what to do. When told what to do, they will feel "judged."
Let's take a look at the scriptures.

Matthew 7:1-2:
"Judge not, that you be not judged. For with what judgement you judge, you will be judged, and with the measure you use, it will be measured back to you."

This scripture is a common scripture used when speaking of judging. So, should we never judge? If correction is so often considered judgment, how should this be handled?

Jude 1 talks about "having compassion for some and others save with fear, pulling them out of the fire, hating even the garment defiled by the flesh." Imagine that you see a car coming towards someone standing in the street. Can you picture it? The person is walking in the street doing whatever they want to do. They do not see the oncoming car, but you do. You are on the outside looking in. They do not even realize that they are in danger. Everything seems harmless to them. Should you just be silent? Should you just mind your own business? Would they be angry if you told them to get out of the road? Would they be angry if you tried telling them that their life was in danger if they didn't move away from where they were? It is possible that they would be angry out of their own ignorance. Honestly, we should all be willing to consider what someone else says. We should take the time to ponder what has been said to see if maybe there is some merit to it. A humble heart will be willing to listen. Now imagine this, what if a person had lost their will to live. Maybe they knew their life was heading down a bad road and they really didn't care. They just wanted to live their own life how they saw fit. Should we just be silent? Their life is their life, right? It isn't fun to be told what to do or to be corrected, but sometimes it is necessary. We are not called to go around getting into everybody's business, but there are times when we are called to do what we can to pull people out of the fire. Sometimes someone must care even if they don't care about themselves. But while we are doing some correcting, we should also be doing some self-evaluating.

Matthew 7:3-5
"And why do you look at the speck in your brother's eye, but do not consider the plank in your own eye? Or how do you say to your brother, 'Let me remove the speck from your eye', and look, a plank is in your own eye? Hypocrite! First remove the plank from your own eye, and then you will see clearly to remove the speck from your brother's eye."

What needs to happen here? We might see someone walking in error or not quite living how they should. It is sometimes easier to see things in others than to see it in ourselves. If we see something in others and we are quick to point it out, we might find ourselves out to be a hypocrite. Isn't a hypocrite someone that does the same thing or similar thing as they accuse someone else of? Have you ever had someone talk about how someone else wasn't much of a Christian because they said this or that; yet the accusing person has said far worse things? What about different addictions? Someone who frequently drinks alcohol might be ok with alcohol but look down on someone that does drugs. Someone that has had sex before marriage might look down on someone that commits adultery. Someone that has had multiple sexual partners might look down on someone that is homosexual. Sin is sin. Period.

    I recently heard a story of someone that was in a homosexual relationship for years and her mother told her she needed to get out of her lifestyle, and she replied that she would when her mother quit smoking. Wow! The mother was telling her daughter something that was truth and something she needed to do; yet the daughter saw her mother doing something for years that she also needed to quit. The amazing thing is that her mother quit smoking, cold turkey, that week. The mother heard her daughter, and as hard as it must have been to stop her addiction, she did what she needed to do. This wasn't something that could be used against her again. No one is perfect, but it is important that our own selves are clean of anything that would hinder our testimony. Sometime after this mother quit smoking, her daughter did get out of the lifestyle she was in. If we want to see a change in others, we need to always make sure we are working on ourselves. We can be pointing out a speck in someone else's eye all while having a plank in our own eye. No one likes a hypocrite, and most people do not even want to hear what they have to say. If our words are going to carry weight, we must be living what we say. When we have struggled with things ourselves, we should have more compassion for others. Even if we haven't struggled with certain things, we should still have compassion because we never know when that could have been or could one day be us. It could be our own friends or family. Life is hard. None of us know the things that we might face one day or how we will handle them. It is often said that God will not put more on us than we can handle. This simply isn't true. If we could handle everything, we wouldn't need God. In 2 Corinthians 1, Paul talks about their sufferings. He explains how they were burdened above their own strength. They felt like they would even die. It was too much for them to handle. These things caused them to rely on the Lord instead of themselves. When our own attitude is one of humility, we will be quick to make sure we, ourselves, are right in those areas first. Then, we will be able to see clearly to remove the speck from our brother's eye. This is where we are given the right to speak what needs to be spoken.

    1 Corinthians 5 speaks about immorality within the church. This was those that professed to be believers; yet they were not living as Christians should live. Paul tells them to not keep company with anyone named a brother (a fellow-Christian), who is sexually immoral, or covetous, or an idolater, or a reviler, or a drunkard, or an extortioner. These are not character traits of a Christian. Christians are not called to be sexually immoral, greedy, idolizing things above God, speaking and spewing abusive language, getting drunk, or robbing and cheating people. This is the type of Christians that Paul warned them to separate from. It goes on to say, "For what have I to do with judging those also who are outside? Do you not judge those who are inside? But those who are outside God judges. Therefore put away from yourselves the evil person." That

is a hard thing to swallow. There are people that consider themselves Christians that habitually live in these ways, and these are people that we love. We don't want them to live in these ways, but these things were not to be tolerated. The sin of a believer was to be taken seriously. We can expect those that are without Christ to live contrary to the Word of God, but those that are within the body should be living differently. God's word has created a standard. God judges those that are outside, but we have been given the job of judging those that are inside. If we are living a life amongst believers that begin to participate in any of the above activities, it is our job to address those things. We are not called to be a part of those activities, nor should we just accept their own standard. The standard of the Bible remains. We can continue to show love, all while speaking the truth. There are times when truth spoken might not seem like love to those that do not want to hear it, but truth still needs to be spoken. Before even speaking, it is always a good idea to pray about the situation and for the person. Covering them in prayer, praying how we should address things, and correct timing is also vitally important. The goal is to see a change of heart. Jesus always makes a way to turn around and come back. Many people that consider themselves Christians have begun to overlook some things. It seems that the Bible is stricter on things than we are these days. Even recently, there have been many ministers and those in ministry that have fallen into embarrassing, wrongful behaviors. Maybe if they had been confronted early on, they could have been helped, or maybe they would have continued in their behavior anyway, but at least they couldn't say that someone didn't warn them. Confronting wrongful behavior isn't fun, but at times, it is necessary. We are called to live a clean life. Keep the log out of your own eye so that you can effectively judge to remove the speck from another's eye.

10
RESTORING WHAT WAS STOLEN

Even though restoration can be a beautiful thing, there are times when restoration may not be an option. Forgiveness is required, but restoration is conditional. A lot of factors must be considered for restoration to take place. Restoration will only be able to be achieved if both parties involved are willing to work at it. Relationships are not meant to be one-sided. One person can work themselves almost to death trying to make things work and it will not be enough, unless the other person decides to participate. Two willing hearts can make any kind of relationship beautiful with time and consistency. Sometimes questions need to be asked. The standard needs to be made clear and there needs to be mutual agreement. A lot of honest conversation is also needed. Each person must be willing to be accountable for their actions and reactions. God created us for relationships. Jesus died for all mankind in order to restore the broken relationship in the garden. The world is filled with all kinds of relationships: marriage, work, business, family, parental, friendship and church relationships. We aren't called to just be sitting on an island somewhere all alone. After a while, complete solitude would get lonely, even though quiet time alone is very inviting. Aah! If any of you are like me, an introvert by heart, solitude does sound amazing at times. It's actually easy to enjoy my own company. I enjoy the quiet. There's just something about a drama free life. Every life has its own problems at times and each day can bring troubles, but there is still peace that comes when there is peace within us. We must realize that not everyone has or understands that peace. Some people love drama, or maybe they are just attracted to it. Drama just follows them around. It's like they are at war all the time. Many times, they are just at war within themselves. Relationships are work. When we are at peace with our own selves, it is easy to get along with ourselves. When we add another person or persons into the equation, it can get a little messy. We all have different ways of doing things. We are all raised under different backgrounds and with different personalities. What seems right to one person might not seem right to another. One person might not think anything of saying or doing something while another person might be greatly offended by it. If nothing is said, how is a person to know that someone is offended? Until you really get to know someone, you might not be aware of the things that trigger them. It takes time and conversation to get to know people. What might seem like a horrible thing to one person, even though maybe not appropriate and somewhat rude, still might not be some great sin. Even Jesus called people names that others would have considered offensive.

    Years ago, I had a dream about an apple that had fallen off of a desk. I was worried that I had done something wrong even though I hadn't done anything in the dream to make it fall. In this dream, a pastor I knew asked if the apple had been broken or bitten into. I looked at the apple and saw that even though it had fallen off of the desk, it was still intact. There is debate as to what kind of fruit was eaten in the garden of Eden, but the apple is commonly used as a symbol of that fruit which can represent sin. I felt like the Lord showed me that I didn't need to worry about saying or doing the wrong thing if it wasn't an actual sin. We live in a society where people are offended over the slightest things. Everyone has an opinion, yet no one else is allowed to have an opinion. If you say something that they consider to be hurtful, they act like you have committed some unforgiveable sin. To disagree with them is to be an enemy. Having relationships can feel like walking on eggshells because of people being so easily offended. The Bible clearly tells us that many will be offended as it gets closer to Jesus' coming. People will betray and hate one another. False prophets will deceive and mislead many (Matthew 24:10,11). It seems like our society has gotten so thin-skinned. People hear what they want to hear and believe what they want to believe. If we are going to survive, we need to toughen up. If we cannot handle it now, how will we handle whatever the future holds? The devil runs rampant, and people let him. He destroys relationships, and people just accept it. The devil is patient and strategic in his planning. He works his destruction and uses people to do his work. We are on a training ground, and we are given tests. We are given the option of playing in the hand of the enemy or the hand of the Lord. Think of Peter. Jesus asks His disciples who people were saying that He was. Peter responded correctly by saying, "You are the Christ, the Son of the living God" (Matthew 16:16). But then a few scriptures down Peter is rebuked and told, "Get behind Me, Satan! You are an offense to Me, for you are not mindful of the things of God, but the things of men" (Matthew 16:23). In one breath his voice is being used to speak the things of God and in another, he is speaking the things of Satan. Satan will do anything he can to influence our thinking. He uses the power of persuasion and is a master manipulator. This is why we must draw closer to the Lord. It's important to continue to fill our mind with good things, daily. We cannot afford to give the enemy any leeway. If he is going to be strategic, we have got to be that much more strategic. Our hearts will need to be enlarged, again and again. Remember, we are not fighting against flesh and blood. If the enemy has his way, there will not be any room for restoration. He wants to cause pain. He gets pleasure out of brokenness and separation. But our great Lord and Savior, Jesus, has made a way back. He comes to repair what was stolen. He comes to heal the broken hearted and heal their wounds. You are not alone. It might be nice to be away from people at times, even Jesus got alone, but we are still created for relationships. Jesus wants to mend what was broken.

He is there for you. He knows your pain, and He aches with you. When people sin against you, they are actually sinning against God Himself. I've seen it. When you do what is right and someone spiritually stabs you in the back, they are actually doing it to God. He takes wrongdoings seriously. It's important to handle things right for ourselves and seek the face of God on how to handle situations. God does not delight in broken relationships. He makes a way to redemption. If you will let Him, He plans to make something beautiful out of the story of your life. That might come in this present life, or it might come hereafter, but it will be made beautiful in time. In Matthew 13 we can read the parable of the wheat and the tare. It tells us a story of a man who sowed good seeds in his field. When the crop appeared, tares also showed up. His servants questioned this because they thought he had sown good seeds. He had, in fact, sown good seeds, but an enemy had also sown tares. He tells his servants, "An enemy has done this" (Matthew 13:28). Some things are out of our control. Some things are not our fault. We are not to be blamed for what has happened. It is an enemy, and we have to decide what to do with that. We have a part to play.

Restoration isn't always easy, and it can be scary. The trust that has been broken doesn't come back quickly restored. Fear can grip you, and worry will try to overtake you. Anxiety will attempt to consume you. You might have to ask yourself some questions. Is this relationship worth restoring? Is this a relationship I want in my life? Am I willing to put in the restoration work? Am I willing to deal with the pain of this restoration? Am I willing to let down my guard and be vulnerable again? Who will be affected if this relationship is or isn't restored? Will I be able to trust again? Will my heart be able to handle this? Can a greater purpose be born out of this? You have to answer these questions for yourself. Really consider your answers. Take time to think about it, and more importantly, take time to pray about it. I do know that the Lord is in the restoration business. The enemy, in his disgusting self and ways, has already done damage, but imagine how different, if given the chance, it can become.

As Jesus hung on the cross, the Bible says He was unrecognizable. Imagine how horrible that looked. Imagine how devastating that was for so many to see. As He hung on that cross, filled with pain, I'm sure it looked hopeless. I'm sure the people that loved Him felt helpless. It was such an injustice, but beauty was in the making. God wasn't finished. Jesus was about to get the reward of His suffering. He was about to fulfill the plan. It was all going to be worth it. He is still waiting for completion, but He's already seeing. My friend, ask yourself the questions. Regardless of your answers, I have no doubt that God is working it out. Take a deep breath and allow your heart to heal. Release those things and people that are out of your control. "Trust in the Lord with all of your heart and lean not on your own understanding; In all your ways acknowledge Him, And He shall direct your paths" (Proverbs 3:5-6). He's working on a plan to restore what the enemy has stolen. The thief will be robbed, and you will receive all that was promised. Take back what was stolen.

11
CONTROL

Wouldn't it be nice if we had more control? Wouldn't it be nice if we could control people's actions and reactions? Wouldn't it be nice if we could zap people if they started making bad choices? Is it just me or does that sound like a great idea? It might sound good as long as we are not the one being zapped. I am joking about zapping, of course, but it seems like a lot of harm could be avoided and a lot of pain eradicated, not only for them and ourselves, but for others also if we could choose for them. In a world where there is free will, we are not called to control others; we are called to control ourselves. Now we do have our legal system that is set up in America to incarcerate those who are out of control and have been convicted of dangerous, illegal, and harmful crimes towards others; certain behaviors can lead people to confined places. We each have a right to be protected from those behaviors.

> **CERTAIN BEHAVIORS CAN LEAD PEOPLE TO CONFINED PLACES**

If we want to maintain our freedom, we must choose self-control. Not everyone will choose to do the right thing on their own.

Judges 17:6 says:
"In those days there was no king in Israel; everyone did what was right in his own eyes."

Can you imagine how life would be if everyone did what was right in their own eyes? Sadly, the world isn't short on evil already, but if there were no consequences for evil or no ruling king, there is no telling what people would be willing to do. The laws set in place are meant to enforce and encourage some kind of self-control. The Bible gives us instructions that are meant to lead us in a path of moral character; those instructions and our desires might not always line up. Paul talks about the war of sin within himself. He said he didn't do the right things that he wanted to do, but he did do the things that he hated (Romans 7:15). He wanted to do what was good, but he didn't. He didn't want to do what was wrong, but he did it anyway. He knew that there was another power at war within his mind. That power seeks to make us a slave to sin.

The movie *Nefarious* gives a vivid picture of this very thing. The main character in the movie has been incarcerated for being a convicted serial killer. On the day of his scheduled execution, he talks with a psychiatrist. As he is being interviewed, a demon talks through him using his voice. The demon has used his body to destroy his life and also the lives of others. Such a sad thing to watch. Even though this man had taken the lives of others, he himself had lost his own life to the will of the demon. The man had become a slave to the demon and his own selfish desires. Even though it's a movie, this is a reality for many. There can be good and evil at work within each of us, and we will be a slave to whatever or whoever we yield to. The evil agenda of the enemy is to control our very nature while the righteous fruit of the Holy Spirit is to bring us to a place of self-control. A person can feel like they are in control while controlling people or situations, but many times that person is actually being controlled themselves. Often, they are being controlled by their own fear, anger, rage, bitterness, unforgiveness, resentments, insecurities, or need for power. There is a difference between leading and controlling. A leader sets an example that people want to follow while a person that seeks to control needs to control in order to get people to comply. One glorifies God and one glorifies the enemy. Our life will speak, but what is it speaking? I don't think anyone has ever had a desire to grow up to be a serial killer, a murderer, rapist, thief, prostitute, or drug dealer. I don't think anyone has ever wanted to be a professional liar, manipulator, or con artist. One thing leads to another and before they know it, they are giving in to something other than what they were created to be; they begin living a life far from what God intended. It's tragic and heartbreaking. When we hear of someone committing horrific crimes, we can understandably feel that they need to suffer for what they have done. Proverbs 6:16 lists 6 things that God hates and 7 that are an abomination to him:

"a proud look, a lying tongue, hands that shed innocent blood, a heart that devises wicked plans, feet that are swift in running to evil, a false witness that speaks lies, and one who sows discord among the brethren."

God hates these things. God hates the works of the enemy. But I remember the Lord speaking to me one day and asking me a few questions. It went something like this:

What if no one prays for them?

What if your prayers caused them to turn around?

What if someone's prayers got them to a place where they never desired to commit those crimes again?

What if someone's prayers brought them to a place of true repentance?

What if they changed to where they never harmed anyone else again?

We can feel like some people are without hope of ever changing, but I often think, what if that was my son or daughter? What if it was someone you or I had cared for, raised, and given our entire life to? Wouldn't we want them to turn around? Wouldn't we want them to never repeat those things again? Wouldn't we want others to never have to worry about being harmed by them? What if Jesus thought we weren't worth dying for or there was no place for our redemption? The truth is, either the devil is winning, or God is winning. There are only two sides to this. We often seek justice, but what if part of that justice was seeing the perpetrator changed? Truly set free and changed. A soul set free from the control of demonic forces is a slap in the face to the devil and a win for the kingdom of God. It is God's gentleness that makes us great, not His harshness.

Recall the story of Jonah and his trip to Nineveh. Jonah was to go to Nineveh to give them word of their coming destruction. In Jonah's disobedience, he fled from his assignment, was swallowed by a great fish, and then vomited up after he repented. Jonah felt that the city of Nineveh deserved their punishment for their evil ways, but they too repented. They cried out to God for forgiveness, and the Lord changed His mind from destruction to life. It was nice for Jonah when his prayers got answered while he was in the deepest, darkest place of the fish's belly, but he felt like it was a different story for Nineveh to be extracted from their own state of darkness. Isn't that the goal - for each of us to be set free from the deepest, darkest hell, to escape the grip of Satan and his little minions so that the kingdom of darkness is defeated, and the kingdom of light shines forth? How does it ever benefit the kingdom of God for the kingdom of Hell to be more populated? Wasn't Hell created for the devil and his angels?

Now I am not going to even pretend that any of this is easy. There are things in life that I hope and pray that my family or I will never have to experience. I'm not sure how I would initially handle certain things. It would be wonderful if we were already living in a peaceful, loving place that was God-fearing and demon free, but that isn't our current reality. It will be our reality one day, but for now, remember to take it one day at a time. One day and then the next, with lots of prayer and dependency on the Holy Spirit. We can't do anything on our own. We could wish more evil on someone that hurt us, but what would that do? Wouldn't it just create more evil? We can't leave room in our heart for that. We are the temple of the Holy Spirit, and we have to be careful what we allow in our own hearts. If it were up to me, we would already be living in a perfect world. Some things are just going to take some time. My heart breaks for the evil that some have had to endure. Some things are just out of our control while others use their control to cause damage, evil, and destruction. I'm sure you have seen that familiar cartoon picture of a devil on one side and an angel on the other whispering into a person's ear. It can be like that. Something is trying to persuade us into complying with its wishes. The flesh and the spirit war against each other just as demons and the Holy Spirit war for the souls of people. I believe that God speaks convictions to people as a warning that they overlook. We've all been guilty of it. In all of that, I also know that God is a healer to the brokenhearted. Something that He shouldn't even have to do, but nonetheless, He knows how to bring healing to devastation. Demons will have their day of judgment. One day every tear will be wiped away, but until then, we continue on. We do what we can in our own limited strength, drawing on the Holy Spirit for His strength, to control ourselves. The Holy Spirit doesn't leave us helpless or comfortless. You can do this. Partner with the Holy Spirit. Invite Him to help you do what you can't. Ask for His help.

Let's look at *Proverbs 16:32:*
"He who is slow to anger is better than the mighty, and he who rules his spirit than he who takes a city."

And also, Proverbs 25:28:
"Whoever has no rule over his own spirit Is like a city broken down, without walls."

At the end of the day, you might not be in control of every situation or every person, but you can be in control of your own vessel. There is power in controlling self. A person who rules his own spirit is mightier than someone who takes a city. Without ruling our own spirit, we are like a city broken down without walls. What good would a house or city be without walls? Any invading thing could come in. We would be left under the influence of whatever wanted to steal from us or take advantage of us.

We can be a person that is out of control and always choosing to control everyone else, or we can be a person of self-control. One will lead to bondage and the other will lead to freedom. It is a great feeling to be self-controlled. On the days that you miss it, ask for forgiveness and help to get back on track. God's mercies are new every morning, and there will be days that we need it. Let the fruit of the Holy Spirit become a part of who you are. Let it grow and thrive in you. Become a place with protective walls that can't be shaken. Embrace self-control so you don't get out of control.

12
FROM DEATH UNTO LIFE

Many things in life just do not make sense. No matter how we try to make sense of them, it just doesn't. I hate sickness, disease, and death. I hate every part of them. Even though there is suffering, pain, and sorrow in the world we live in, I still believe and have seen that Jesus heals today. I know that there is a place of healing, and I also know that death is inevitable. We will all face death. Death is hard at any age, and we are never really prepared to say goodbye, but when someone dies young it just seems a little more devastating. It can seem so unfair. It just seems like everyone should get to live out a long life, but not everyone is given that. Every life has a purpose and sometimes that purpose is cut shorter than we imagined.

When my sweet momma was given the diagnoses of breast cancer, I never expected it to take her life. Never. It really didn't even cross my mind that within a year or so she would be gone. She was one of the kindest, most unselfish people that I ever knew. She gave her entire life to her family. She lived a very simple life and seemed very content with what she had. I never heard her complain. I'm sure there were days when she did, like we all have a tendency of doing, but I don't remember her complaining. Even in her pain with cancer and treatment, she didn't complain to me. I think she just didn't want me to worry. She put others before herself, and she loved deeply from her heart. She did everything she could to rise above her own childhood life to give us a better one, she and our daddy both. We might not have grown up in some big, fancy house, but we never went without. We had everything we needed and other things that we wanted. Daddy worked very hard to provide for us, and Momma made sure the house trailer was clean. We always had food to eat and decent clothes to wear. She made it a real place of home. She was a true Momma at heart. I knew she loved me. She might not have spoken it a lot with words, but her life showed it. I remember vividly the day she taught me unconditional love. I didn't understand it at the time, and I do not even think she knew the example she had set, but now I understand completely. It was a love straight from the heart of God. It was a love that pushed past her own feelings. It was a committed love, "a no matter what" kind of love. I am forever thankful for that kind of love. That day her heart was enlarged. She helped me more than she ever knew. Leaving this earth at the age of 41 was just too young. I needed her and still miss her terribly at times, but I know she is much better off than we are. In my own selfishness, I'd like her to still be here, but I know I'll see her again. The Lord has a way of comforting us when we seek Him. Even though I hate death with a passion, death has taught me a few things. My brokenness over loss led me to the feet of Jesus. I didn't have anywhere else to go. Thankfully, alcohol and drugs were never a part of my life. I had no numbing agent. Depending on Jesus became my numbing agent. He was the only One that could get me through. I had a lot of questions, and He could handle those questions. Don't be afraid to ask. You may or may not get an answer or the answer that you want, but it's ok to ask. Some people believe that we are never to question God, but I've seen that to be wrong. I've asked, and He has answered. One of the questions I had for God was, "Why did you take my momma when there are far worse people in the world?" It seemed to me that if someone was going to die it shouldn't be someone with such a good heart. The world needs more people like that, not less. His response was that He sometimes leaves the bad ones in order to give them time to change and be saved. I didn't like that answer, but I could be at peace with that. Momma's death really woke up our entire family to the fragileness of life. In her death, I believe it caused many of us to turn to God more. As strange as it might sound, her death caused the Devil to lose. It became our wake-up call, and she was no longer suffering.

    I grieved really hard for 3 years. I cried many tears, and finally complete peace filled my heart. I remember one day in prayer that the Lord gave me a vision of Momma in heaven. To make things clear for those that do not understand visions, this wasn't something I was seeking. I do not believe we should seek the dead. Seeking the dead in the Bible is called necromancy. This is forbidden. We are not to seek the dead. We are not to seek psychics, witches, warlocks, or mediums in order to seek the dead. We are to seek

Jesus, and when we seek Him, He can at times reveal things to us that bring comfort, strength, and peace. Part of my healing process came because the Lord allowed me to see things as I looked to Him in prayer. The Lord speaks to those that seek Him and are willing to take the time to listen.

Back to the vision.

In this vision, she had her arms in a jogging position, surrounded by clouds, smiling, and I had the thought of her saying, "Keep on running." It's like she was looking down at me. Seeing her like that was amazing. She looked so full of life and at peace. As I'm seeing this, I was reminded of a scripture in the Bible about the cloud of witnesses.

Hebrews 12:1-2:
"Therefore we also, since we are surrounded by so great a cloud of witnesses, let us lay aside every weight, and the sin which so easily ensnares us, and let us run with endurance the race that is set before us, looking unto Jesus, the author and finisher of our faith, who for the joy that was set before Him endured the cross, despising the shame, and has set down at the right hand of the throne of God."

At that time in my walk with the Lord, I was somewhat aware of this scripture, but just assumed that this only referred to Abraham, Isaac, Jacob or other old-time saints of the Bible. As I was seeing this vision and getting this understanding, I remember telling myself that I knew I wasn't just imagining this. It seemed so real. After looking the scripture up in my Bible about the cloud of witnesses, I was amazed to see that it said to "run" with endurance the race that is set before us. It said to run, and that is exactly what I saw Momma doing. She was encouraging me to keep running. As all of this is coming together, I am in shock and awe of the Lord. Not only did I see Momma, but I also saw Pawpaw Herbert there near her. He had passed away 4 years after her. He had been in a war in his earlier days, and as a kid, I remember him drinking alcohol a lot. It seemed like he always had a beer in his hand or close by. I think that his time in the war was probably a great part of his alcohol addiction. It is a shame that the alcohol stole so much of his life from him. He had the sweetest smile and the kindest heart. I think he would have given the shirt off of his back to anyone that needed it. I truly loved him and thought highly of him. He ended up getting sick and basically became bedridden. We had already had a planned vacation to an out-of-state church camp meeting. I knew he was sick, but I didn't realize how close to death he actually was. I never expected him to pass while I was gone, but something strange happened. At the end of one of the church meetings I became very upset. I felt a strong urge to pray. I began praying, interceding, and crying. I really didn't know exactly what it was all about. I did hear the Lord say that my pawpaw would walk again. Most of my prayer was in tongues. As I continued to pray, a lady came up to me to tell me that she had never done anything like that before, but she felt strongly to come pray for me. I do not remember exactly what she prayed, but I knew I felt more peaceful. After this, I still felt like I needed to continue praying, so I did. It was just minutes later that my husband came to tell me that he had gotten a call that Pawpaw Herbert had passed on. Just at the time that the Lord had me praying, and sent someone to pray for me, back in Louisiana Pawpaw was passing on without me even knowing it. Only God! What is even more amazing is in the second half of my vision, my pawpaw was smiling, and I had the thought of him saying, "Thank you for praying for me." It seemed like the strangest thing. As I was seeing this vision, I was reminded of the time back at the camp meeting when the Lord had me interceding. It still blows my mind thinking of how good God is that he allowed me to be praying at the time of his passing. What if I had ignored that burden of prayer? I later realized that when the Lord said he would walk again, it was in Heaven and not on this Earth. People will believe what they want to believe, but that vision and experience caused me to give glory to God, and for whatever reason, Pawpaw Herbert needed that prayer as he was moving on.

There have been several deaths that really had an impact on me. One of those was the death of my Uncle Ivy. He passed on in January of 2019. Growing up he was only about 6 years older than me. He seemed more like an older brother. With him living right next door to us, I saw him more often. I remember him playing basketball with us in the circle or baseball many times out in the back yard. Some people leave us with fond memories in our minds without them even trying. I remember as we got older, he was the one at family functions that was always cracking jokes. You never knew what he might say. While it seemed to me like most people in the family were more serious and quieter by nature, he was the life of the party. He made life interesting. We laughed sometimes so hard that it hurt. As he got older, I didn't see him as much. At one point he got very involved in church, which made me very happy. I believe he was faithful to what he knew. Even though I love church, I hate religion. In the name of Jesus, religion destroys many. What seems to be taking someone somewhere is actually just keeping them bound. I know some will be angry about this, but no one denomination is "the" one denomination. If you think that your group or your denomination has all the answers, you are sadly mistaken. Some people seem to think that their own group is some elite group that is superior to all of the others. Obviously, we are going to gravitate to a denomination or body of believers that we feel have the most truth and hopefully we are all searching out the scriptures of the Bible to see for ourselves, but no one group has all of the answers. We have many denominations, but there will only be one kingdom in Heaven. There isn't going to be a Heaven just for Baptist, Pentecostals, Presbyterian, Charismatics, etc. Jesus is God over people, but not God over just one religious denomination. I remember at one point my uncle told me, "Just between me and you, I think your momma went to Heaven." At this point I had already had the vision of my momma, so I had every confidence, comfort, and knowing that she had made it. I remember telling him that I knew she had made it. You see, he said this because his religious teaching taught him that those that do not speak in tongues do not go to Heaven, and he knew that Momma didn't speak in tongues. According to what he was taught, she wouldn't have made it to Heaven, but in his heart, he believed that she did. His teaching didn't line up with his "knowing" inside. A relationship with Jesus isn't the same as following manmade rules of religion. Sadly, he found this out after his death and not before.

Even though I had the gift of speaking in tongues, which according to his church's teachings, qualified me for Heaven, I still wore makeup and cut my hair which were forbidden according to his religion. I remember him telling me that I would be judged for cutting my hair. If I truly believed this to be true, I wouldn't have cut it, but I knew he was just going off of what he had been taught. He was very passionate about his religious beliefs, and even though I didn't agree with all of what he was being taught, I do believe that he loved Jesus. I prayed for him a lot. I'm not sure what happened, but sometime later he got away from church. From what I understand, he got into a life of addiction. He went in the total opposite direction. Then one day I saw him as I was leaving my dad's house. He had lost a lot of weight, his face looked skinny, but he still smiled as he saw me with the same friendly personality. We had a quick conversation. I do not remember exactly what he said, but he made a comment of needing something or needing to do something, and I remember vividly saying, "What you need is Jesus." He responded, "Amy, you are right about that." This was the last time I saw him until I saw him in the hospital. My dad had told me that he had been admitted. According to the doctors, he had bleeding on his brain. I hated seeing him like that. I had hopes of him making it out of that hospital. Before we left that day, he was good with us praying for him. I remember praying that this wasn't the life that God had for him. I also remember feeling real peace about his salvation. It was another week before I went back with Daddy to see him. I knew at this point that it didn't look good. His urine bag had a lot of blood in it. He just laid there. I questioned if they were giving him fluids or food. They weren't giving him anything. It seemed like he just laid there dying. I was really upset that nothing was being done. It just seemed so wrong! I kept praying for him after that visit. Then the night before he passed on, I awoke during the night feeling an urge to get up to pray. As I prayed in tongues, I could hear English in my mind. I knew this was not about me. I realized that the Holy Spirit was praying through me for Ivy. It was a prayer to forgive those that had hurt him and even a prayer to forgive the doctors and nurses for what they were allowing to happen to him. I believe, with the right care, he might have made it out of that hospital. I know that not everyone will agree with that, but I know that the Holy Spirit was revealing things to me in that prayer. The next day I found out that he had passed on. I felt so sad about the entire situation. My heart felt heavy.

    I do want to add something right here. It can be heartbreaking to see someone lie there and suffer. For some people, it might seem that God isn't a good God to allow someone to suffer like that instead of just letting them pass on, but I do believe that sometimes it is actually the mercy of God giving them a chance to prepare their heart. As they seem to be unresponsive, their spirit is still very much alive. This can give them time to forgive others, seek forgiveness for themselves, and call out to God. Sometimes they might need that time to let go, or it could allow time for family to prepare their own heart for the departure. Some people die more instantly, and others are given more time. Either way, a lot can happen in those seconds, minutes, hours, or days before passing on. As the two thieves hung on the cross with Jesus, they each had a space of time to repent. As they were still hanging on to life, one of them chose to take that time to believe. As he accepted Jesus, Jesus promised him that he would be with Him that day in paradise (Luke 23:43). That time for him was crucial and precious.

The Sunday after Ivy passed, I was up front at church worshipping. Out of nowhere, I had a quick vision. I saw Ivy lying face down on what looked like a stage. It was such a bright, radiant light that glowed like I had never seen before. As I see him lying there, I hear the Holy Spirit say, "He is going to cry for three days." I was shocked. I didn't understand what this meant. It troubled me every day that week. I sought the Lord on it over and over again in prayer. I only told my husband and daughters. I wanted to know what this meant. Our oldest daughter said that maybe it was about his salvation, but I said no because I believed that was a decision he had to make before dying, and I had already had peace about that.

As I kept asking the Lord, I felt like He answered. I wasn't sure why it was specifically three days, but the Lord showed me that he was weeping over his life. He was weeping over all of the things that he could have done and should have done. He was weeping over ruining his testimony. He was weeping over his choices and his lack of understanding. I was so shocked and amazed at the Lord for allowing me to see this. It made so much sense. It made me sad because I knew it could have been different, but it gave me peace in knowing that his heart was crying out and his eyes had been opened. He was seeing what he didn't see before. He was being healed from what he couldn't heal from before. God was doing a work in him that had never been done before. There are things from this life that he just couldn't keep with him in his new life.

Now, six years later, I feel like I have a better understanding of those three days. Recently, while in the process of writing this book and listening to the Bible audibly, I heard it mention three days. It caught my attention. I began looking up things that happened in the Bible on the third day. I had never paid much attention to the number of things that have been listed as happening on the third day.

Here are some mentions of three days from the Bible:
1. Jesus was buried and rose again on the third day (1 Corinthians 15:4).

2. Jesus was at the wedding in Cana on the third day where He performed His first miracle (John 2:1).
3. Jonah was delivered out of the mouth of the great fish after three days and three nights (Jonah 1:17; Jonah 2:10).
4. Hezekiah's prayers were heard, and his tears were seen by the Lord. The Lord said that Hezekiah would go up to the temple of the Lord on the third day and be healed (2 Kings 20:5).
5. Esther approached the King to save her people on the third day of their fast (Esther 5:1-2).

Just reading these scriptures opened my eyes. Here we have resurrection, a miracle, deliverance, healing, and salvation all on the third day. This is what seemed to have been happening to Ivy on that third day in Heaven. God was giving him life again, healing his soul, delivering and saving him from the pain of his past mistakes and disappointments.

Then I read *Hosea 6:2:*
"After two days He will revive us; On the third day He will raise us up, that we may live in His sight."

Ivy already knew of his need for Jesus as Savior before he died. He had already accepted that salvation, but there was still work to be done. I believe the Lord revived him and on that third day, he was raised up to live in the Lord's sight. All things were being made new. God sure is faithful, and I am so grateful!

I continued to ponder what I had seen all that next week. It stayed in my heart and on my mind. Then the next Sunday I went up front for worship again. Without even trying to see anything, I had a second vision. I saw Ivy in Heaven wearing an all-white suit holding up a silver cup. It looked like some kind of communion cup. As he held the cup up, I had the thought of him saying, "I never knew it could be that way." In my mind I thought, "I know". And then I had the thought of him saying back, "No, I really never knew it could be that way!" My heart felt broken because I realized that he was talking about communion with the Lord. On this Earth, he understood religion, but he didn't really understand relationship with God. His understanding was limited to what he had been taught. He really didn't know that it could be that way. He didn't know he could have real communion with the Lord here on earth. He had missed out on so much. I think this is why his walk with the Lord wasn't sustainable. Even though he had been excited about the Lord at one point, it wasn't lasting. I think it was too hard to live what he was trying to live. If he had known then what he was learning now, I think his life would have been different. There is so much that we all do not completely understand. We see through a glass darkly and then face to face. None of us have all of the answers. That face-to-face clarity would make all the difference. This vision really opened up my understanding, and it caused me to look at my own walk with the Lord differently. Up to this point I had grown in the Lord, continued to study, read the Word, pray, and seek God, but this brought a whole new seriousness about my time here on Earth. It changed my entire life honestly. I can never look at this life the same again. Time is short and decisions are serious. I continued to think about these things, over and over again. I questioned if I could possibly do enough for the Lord. I questioned what my life would speak of at the end of my days. I questioned if I would fulfill my assignment here on Earth. I questioned if I would ever do even half of what the Lord originally wanted or planned for me before I was formed in my mother's womb. It seemed overwhelming and convicting all at once. It drove me to a greater determination about this life. How could I ever look at life the same again? The truth is, I can't. It blessed me and wrecked me all at the same time. I see others living their life without even thinking of eternity or at least not taking it thoughtfully. Sometimes I wish I could live like that, but knowing what I know, I can't. If my life is being written in a book, I want it to speak volumes. I want it to be a story that brought people hope, pointed them to truth, and made them feel loved. I want it to be a story without regrets. Long after I am gone, I want my story to keep speaking. More than anything else, I want to hear, "Well done, good and faithful servant." One thing I know is that even though Ivy had regrets, his life and story spoke volumes to me, and it can keep speaking to those that have ears to hear.

  The next week I continued to think about these things. Sunday came around again and this time I asked the Lord to let me see a vision of Ivy one more time. And you know, He was faithful. As I worshipped, I had a vision of Ivy with a white cloth around his shoulders and over his head. He was smiling and worshipping a crazy kind of worship. It brought the biggest smile to my face! I finally knew that he had not only made it, but he was experiencing real life. He was experiencing the true love of the Father that he longed for. His rejection had been turned into acceptance. His pain, tears, and sorrow had turned to joy. He was experiencing the joy of the Lord as never before, and this time it would last for all of eternity. The redemptive hand of the Lord had welcomed him in and made him whole. I will praise the Lord forever for His unfailing love! With men it may be impossible, but with God all things are possible to those that believe. Hallelujah forever to the King! Some things seek to wreck us, destroy us, and take us out, But God has a greater plan!

If you are reading this book and have never accepted Jesus Christ as your Savior, there is no better time than right now. I hope that you have taken everything that has been said thus far to heart. Life is serious, eternity is real, and you are wanted there. There is a place waiting for you if you choose to accept and believe.

Romans 10:9,10,13:
"That if you confess with your mouth the Lord Jesus and believe in your heart that God raised Him from the dead, you will be saved. For with the heart one believes unto righteousness, and with the mouth confession is made unto salvation. For "whoever calls on the name of the Lord shall be saved."

Salvation isn't hard. Jesus already did the hard work on the cross. He's just waiting on you to accept Him. This can take place wherever you are. If you are ready, from your heart, just begin talking to Him. Ask Him to become a part of your life, to forgive you of any known or unknown sins, and begin walking with you. Whoever calls on the name of the Lord will be saved. Regardless of any past mistakes, sins, or failures, He wants you and loves you. Speak with your mouth and believe in your heart, and you will be saved.

For anyone that just spoke to the Lord from your heart, welcome to the family. All of Heaven is rejoicing with you!

For those that have been on this journey with the Lord, remember that the things we see now are temporary. If we look at the things that are seen, we can fall apart. We must look at the things that are not seen. That's where our focus has to be. Our hearts will have to be enlarged in this life. There will be many times when we have to forgive, let things go, refuse to take things in, and release the pain of what we can't handle on our own. There are things that are just too hard for our small hearts to manage. It is my prayer that something in this book has helped you. It is also my prayer that the Lord will be with you every step of your journey. Life might throw you some very difficult things. You might feel like you just can't continue on at times, but when your heart is enlarged, you will find grace and strength in a time of need. As you hold on, the Lord will use what was meant for evil for your good. When God enlarges your heart, you will become all that you were meant to be.

As I close this book, I leave you with much love and prayers. From one enlarged heart unto another, know that this life might not always be easy, but it will be worth it. Forgive daily and praise often. Do not be afraid when it's time for your heart to be enlarged. An enlarged heart is a growing heart. Daily seek God in prayer. Build a relationship with the Lord and with people.

> HEAVEN AWAITS AND TIME IS SHORT. LIVE A FOCUSED LIFE.

Heaven awaits and time is short. Live a focused life. God is taking you from death unto life so that you might live again.

CONCLUSION

There have been people that have played an integral part in my life here on Earth that are now passed on. None of us know how many years we will be given here. We might not know the day of our death, but we can do something with our life while we're still living. We can impact someone else's life, become the best version of ourselves, and live for more than this world has to offer.

There are people that believe that we just quit existing once we die, and there are others that believe that we are reincarnated as something else. Some people do not believe in Heaven or just believe in Heaven and not Hell. There are people that want to believe that everyone goes to Heaven. If you have ever heard life after death experiences, they all refer to a bright, white, peaceful light or the darkness of a deepest Hell with great torment. There will be two choices. There have been too many people that have experienced these things for it not to be real. Just from the visions I have seen, I know that Heaven is real and there is life after this current one. I cannot express enough how important it is to live our days with purpose. Enjoy your time here on Earth but live for more than just enjoyment and materiel wealth. Life is a beautiful gift that will come with twists and turns. It may come with some extremely hard decisions, but this life is only a small reflection of what is to come. Keep focusing on what really matters. Use your time wisely, find your place, make a difference, and live.

The small trailer church on family property. Momma (front left), me (little girl in front), Mrs. Mildred (Pawpaw's 2nd wife-behind my mom), Aunt Wanda (my dad's sister-center), Pawpaw Herbert (behind my aunt), Brother Matthews (back right).

The black swan my daughter made for me. After all of these years, the purple heart has changed to more of a reddish color.

Momma
and
Daddy

Momma
and Me

Roxanne and Me

Momma
Deborah
(Debbie) Lewis
Hopkins
1957 -1998
Given 41 years
on this Earth

Pawpaw Herbert
Hopkins Sr
1930 – 2002
Given 71 years on
this Earth

Ivy
Ivy Clay
Courtney
1969 -2019
Given 49 years
on this Earth

My Childhood
Best Friend
Christi
Roxanne Reed
1975 – 2022
Given 47
years on this
Earth

ACKNOWLEDGEMENTS

I would like to give special thanks to my friend, Jennifer Ristic, for taking time out of life's busy schedule to read and look over this book. Your encouragement, advice, and time are very much appreciated!

I thank God for those that have created videos and online written information, as well as those that have given verbal information that has helped me with formatting this book. I had no clue what I was doing. You have made this process easier.

I give thanks to my girl, Kailee, for helping with the swan image. You are much smarter than I am.

I give thanks to my husband for helping in the uploading of this book. Your love and support mean so much!

I always thank the Holy Spirit for not only getting me through things that were too hard for me, but for also continuing to be with me, help me, guide me, and change me. I need You every day!

Endnotes

Chapter 2

[i] Purple Heart definition taken online. Accessed on January 6, 2025, https://wwwbritannica.com. Britannica ©2025 Encyclopædia Britannica, Inc.

[ii] Wounded Warrior Regiment Fact Sheet | Purple Heart Released: Benefit6-01-06042015 Accessed on January 6, 2025, www.woundedwarriorregiment.org
Wounded Warrior Regiment
1998 Hill Ave
Quantico, VA 22134

[iii] Black Swan definition taken from Dictionary.com. Accessed on January 6, 2025, © 2024 Dictionary.com, LLC

[iv] Black swan theory from Wikipedia encyclopedia. Accessed on January 6, 2025, https://www.wikipedia.org Wikimedia Foundation, Inc.

Chapter 3

[v] Coward definition taken from Dictionary.com. Accessed on January 6,2025, © 2024 Dictionary.com, LLC

Made in the USA
Columbia, SC
24 April 2025